Conestoga Wagons

BY

RICHARD AMMON

ILLUSTRATED BY

BILL FARNSWORTH

HOLIDAY HOUSE

NEW YORK

Library of Congress Cataloging-in-Publication Data
Ammon, Richard.
Conestoga wagons / by Richard Ammon; illustrated by Bill Farnsworth.—1st ed.
p. cm.
Includes bibliographical references.
Summary: Explains how Conestoga wagons were built and
driven as well as their historical significance and importance
to the early American economy.
ISBN 0-8234-1475-2
1. Wagons—United States—History Juvenile literature.
2. Transportation—United States—History Juvenile literature.
[l. Wagons—History. 2. Transportation—History.]
I. Farnsworth, Bill, ill. II. Title. TS2010.A46 2000
388.3'41—dc21 99-019726

To Jeannie
R. A.

To my wife, Deborah,
and my daughters, Allison and Caitlin
B. F.

The author wishes to thank the following persons
for indispensable help:
Arthur L. Reist, Bruce Bomberger, Kurt Bell, Dave,
and especially Mary Cash

Today the port of Philadelphia bustles as cranes unload cargo from ships onto waiting trucks and trains. In colonial America, when ships with tall masts crowded the docks, that busy scene was not much different.

Between 1750 and 1850, goods were unloaded into

Conestoga wagons, which served as the tractor-trailer trucks of that time.

Built in Lancaster County, Pennsylvania, these heavy-duty wagons were named for the Conestoga Valley, which lies in the heart of Pennsylvania Dutch country.

Some days as many as three thousand Conestoga wagons traveled mostly between Philadelphia and Lancaster, as well as to other Pennsylvania cities to the west: Harrisburg and Pittsburgh. Today U.S. Route 30 and the Pennsylvania Turnpike follow these old wagon trails, which in colonial times were more like rocky paths.

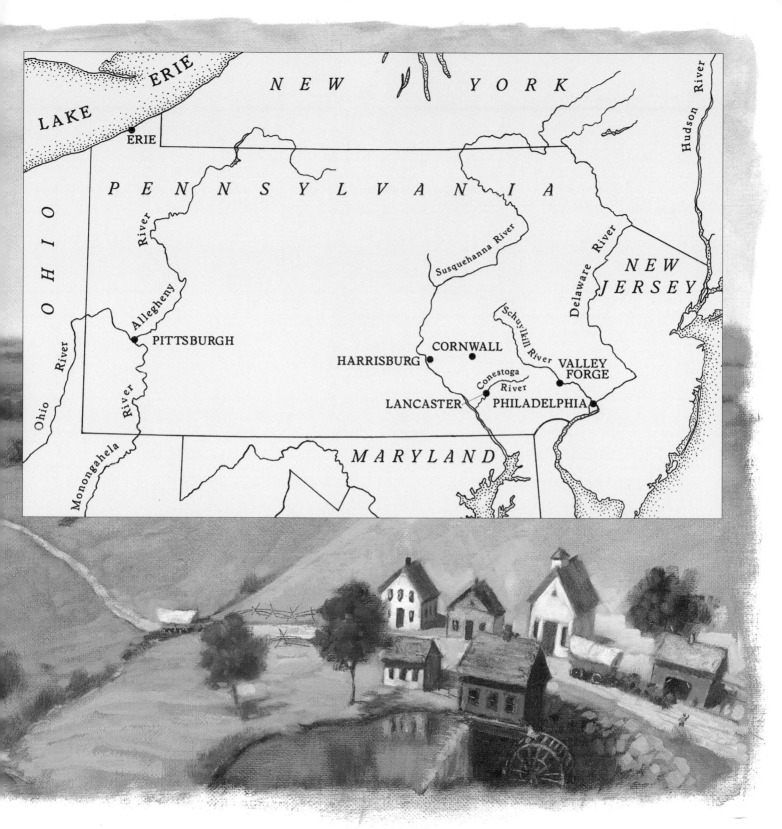

Even for colonial travelers riding in comfortable coaches, a trip over these rugged roads became a bone-jarring experience. In those days there were few bridges, so drivers simply drove their wagons through rivers and streams. Conestoga wagons had to be built sturdy enough to hold together over such rough terrain.

As are so many things today, Conestoga wagons came in three sizes: small, medium, and large. Large wagons could haul as much as five tons, which is the weight of about 160 fourth graders. Smaller wagons carried two to three tons.

Conestoga wagons were not built in factories, as are today's cars and trucks. Rather, they were made by hand. Many were built by blacksmiths, who forged metal and also fitted horses with shoes. Others were built by wainwrights or wagon makers.

While Conestoga wagons were covered, not all covered wagons were Conestogas. One distinguishing feature of Conestoga wagons was the curved oak floor that forced the load toward the center of the wagon. The push toward the center helped to keep cargo such as barrels from rolling around.

The covers, made of homespun linen and waterproofed with linseed oil or beeswax, were draped over anywhere from eight to thirteen bows. These wagons also had an end-gate panel, like the tailgate of a pickup truck, that could be removed for easy loading and unloading.

The hitch was set high to make it easier for the horses to pull their heavy loads. But the height of the wagon could be no higher than men could lift.

Roads in colonial America were not smooth superhighways. They were usually paths with two ruts worn by wagon wheels and a grassy strip in the middle. These roads were often hard and bumpy, but in the spring or after a drenching rain, they turned into a muddy mess.

So wheels on Conestoga wagons needed to be large and strong. The rear wheels had fourteen to sixteen spokes and stood about five to six feet tall. The front wheels were smaller. They had twelve spokes and were about four feet tall.

To make these wheels, the wheelwright hammered the spokes into the holes, called "mortises," around the hub. That was hard work. With all his might, the wheelwright struck the spokes, pounding them into the tight mortises.

The wheels were angled so the part below the axle was pitched inward, while the part above the axle turned outward. When the wagon was filled with freight, the load pushed on the wheels, forcing them upright or vertical.

The wheels were shaped like large dishes or plates, with the spokes spreading from the hub. The rims were made from about seven semicurved sections, called "fellies," that were cut out of plank oak.

Tires on automobiles are filled with air and fit snugly around the wheels. In the 1700s and most of the 1800s, tires were strips of iron wrapped around the wheels. To make them, a blacksmith measured the circumference of the wheel with a tool called a "traveller," which was a small wheel with a handle on it. He counted the number of times the traveller turned around the outside of the wheel, including any fraction of a turn. Then he measured a long, straight ribbon of iron by running his traveller over it. But when he cut the iron, he snipped it three quarters of an inch shorter than the wheel.

To put the tire on the wheel, the blacksmith heated the iron until it glowed red. Then he bent the hot metal and joined the two ends. Because hot metal expands, the shorter tire now fit the wheel.

The moment the blacksmith began hammering the tire on the wheel, smoke and flames danced up from the wooden wheel. With the tire in place, the blacksmith doused the wheel with water, causing the metal to hiss and spit steam. While cooling, the wheel squeaked and groaned as the tire shrank, squeezing and tightening the wheel joints.

In Colonial times no wagons except the Conestogas had brakes. Without brakes, going down a hill with a heavy load was a big problem. To keep other types of wagons from running into the horses or oxen, drivers had to latch chains through the spokes of the wheels and attach the chains to the wagon frame. The locked wheels then skidded down the slope.

But Conestoga wagons were fitted with more advanced mechanisms. While descending a hill, the wagon's driver pulled a five-foot-long iron lever forward that pressed blocks of wood against the wheels and slowed the wagon. To keep the brake on, the teamster fastened a chain on the brake lever to a pin under the wagon.

The hardy men who drove Conestoga wagons were called
teamsters because they drove teams of horses. Today most
truck drivers belong to the Teamsters Union, a union formed
when men drove teams rather than trucks. Unlike modern
truckers in enclosed cabs, the Conestoga drivers walked on
the left side of the wagon beside the front wheels. Because
teamsters worked in every kind of weather, they often wore
buckskins that lasted longer than homespun cloth.

Conestoga wagons were outfitted with several features. To rest, a teamster pulled out an oak board tucked under the wagon in front of the rear wheels. He could ride on this seat known as the "lazy board." Conestoga wagons also carried a feed box for the horses, a jack, and a toolbox. A bucket and tar pot to grease the wheels hung from the sides of the wagons.

Conestoga wagons were pulled by a special breed of draft horses, Conestoga horses. These massive horses measured sixteen to seventeen hands at the withers. (One hand equals four inches.) And they weighed 1,800 pounds or more (the weight of twenty-nine fourth graders). Yet these heavy-duty horses looked somewhat like carriage horses. Since Conestoga wagons often traveled over muddy roads, this special breed had no long hair beneath the fetlocks, the lowest joints on a horse's legs, and no long tails that could become matted. Sadly, these fine workhorses are now extinct.

It took six of these massive horses to pull a Conestoga wagon. The left-hand horse nearest the wagon was called the "wheel horse" or the "saddle horse."

Jerk Line

Off Side Tongue

Off Side Swing

The teamster drove the team by working a single rein
called the "jerk line." To turn the team to the right, the
teamster would yell "Gee" and give several short jerks of the line.
To go left, he would call "Haw" and pull steadily on the jerk line.
Each horse wore a set of bells hanging from an arch that was

Six Horse Hitch

Saddle Horse

Swing Leader

Leader

Off Side Leader

attached to its collar. The horses in front had five bells; those in the middle wore four bells; and those next to the wagon had three bells. These bells announced that the team was coming and that people and cattle should get out of the way. The expression "I'll be there with bells on" comes from this custom.

As the trucks of early America, Conestoga wagons carried
a variety of products. They hauled heavy things, such as coal,
iron, salt, and paper. They carried light things: feathers and
eggs. They carried good things to eat: bacon, butter, cheese,
cider, fish, flour, cornmeal, molasses, salted meat, lard, sugar,
and spices; and things to eat with: knives and forks; things to
wear: buttons, skins, silk, and wool; and other necessities of
life: axes, hemp for making rope, tools, and even mail.

Conestoga wagons also helped shape the history of
America. During the Revolutionary War, they carried grain
and other supplies to Washington's army at Valley Forge and
transported cannons forged at Cornwall, Pennsylvania, to the
camps of the Continental Army.

Later, during the War of 1812, Conestoga wagons transported
loads of gunpowder from the DuPont powder works in
Delaware to American soldiers and sailors at Erie, Pennsylvania.

A Conestoga wagon, loaded with two to five tons of goods, took five days to travel from Philadelphia to Lancaster, a distance of about sixty miles. Of course, this meant that the driver would need to find a place to sleep at night.

In those days, taverns were the hotels and motels of today. These inns played many important roles. During the Revolutionary War, taverns became courtrooms, officers' headquarters, and meeting places for patriots. Thomas Jefferson wrote the Declaration of Independence in the Indian Queen, a Philadelphia tavern.

In colonial days, many people could not read, so taverns hung signs shaped like their names. Some had busts of patriotic heroes, such as Washington, Lafayette, Hancock, Adams, Jefferson, Madison, Monroe, and Franklin. Others looked like objects: The Swan, The Red Lion, The Sign of Ye Hat, The Eagle, The Three Crowns, and The Sign of the Buck.

The Conestoga wagon driver could not stay at just any tavern. Some inns were for rich people traveling by stagecoach, carriages that could race from Philadelphia to Lancaster in one day. These taverns had cozy bedrooms and dining rooms serving delicious meals.

Conestoga wagon teamsters stopped at taverns with names such as Cross Keys, The Wagon, and The Black Bear. These taverns had no bedrooms. The men simply laid out their bedrolls and slept on the barroom floors. In summer the wagoner might sleep near his wagon under the stars.

Whenever a thirsty wagoner ordered beer, the innkeeper would keep a record on a slate by writing "P" for pint or "Q" for quart. When a cheerful wagoner began treating his friends and his tally began mounting, the innkeeper might remind the generous fellow to "mind his P's and Q's," an expression that today is a reminder to mind our manners.

A wagoner's bill for a meal and an overnight stay would total about $1.75. However, the innkeeper would often be happy to barter for whatever the wagoner was carrying: a bundle of wool or flax, or perhaps a slab of salt pork or bacon.

Rules of The Lamp Post

Four pence a night for bed
Six pence with Supper
No more than five to sleep in
   one bed
No boots to be worn in bed
Organ Grinders to sleep in the
   Wash House
No dogs allowed upstairs
No beer allowed in the Kitchen
No Razor Grinders or Tinkers
   taken in

The Conestoga wagon represented the most advanced
technology of its day, with its brakes, lazy board, and sturdiness.
But another technology was developing: the steam engine.
In 1830 a little engine, *The Tom Thumb*, lost a race to a horse
pulling a carriage. But by 1850 locomotives had become so

powerful that, depending upon the size of their engines, they could pull ten to one hundred times that of the Conestogas. These trains raced along at a speed of about ten miles an hour, cutting the travel time from Philadelphia to Lancaster from five days to just one.

Within a few years the Conestogas were no longer used for long-distance hauling. However, until the invention of trucks, Conestoga wagons continued to haul freight from railroad stations to nearby businesses, and other short stretches.

Today you can see a number of original Conestoga wagons
in museums. A few families still own these historic wagons
and drive them on special occasions, keeping alive the memory
of their remarkable contribution to our nation's history.

References

Fisher, Leonard Everett. *The Oregon Trail*. New York: Holiday House, 1990.

Reist, Arthur L. *Conestoga Wagon–Masterpiece of the Blacksmith*. Lancaster, Pennsylvania: Forry and Hacker, 1975.

Shumway, George, and Howard C. Frey. *Conestoga Wagon 1750–1850*. York, Pennsylvania: George Shumway, 1968.

Tunis, Edwin. *Colonial Craftsmen*. Cleveland, Ohio: The World Publishing Company, 1965.

White, John H., Jr. *American Locomotives: An Engineering History, 1830–1880*. Baltimore, Maryland: Johns Hopkins Press, 1968.